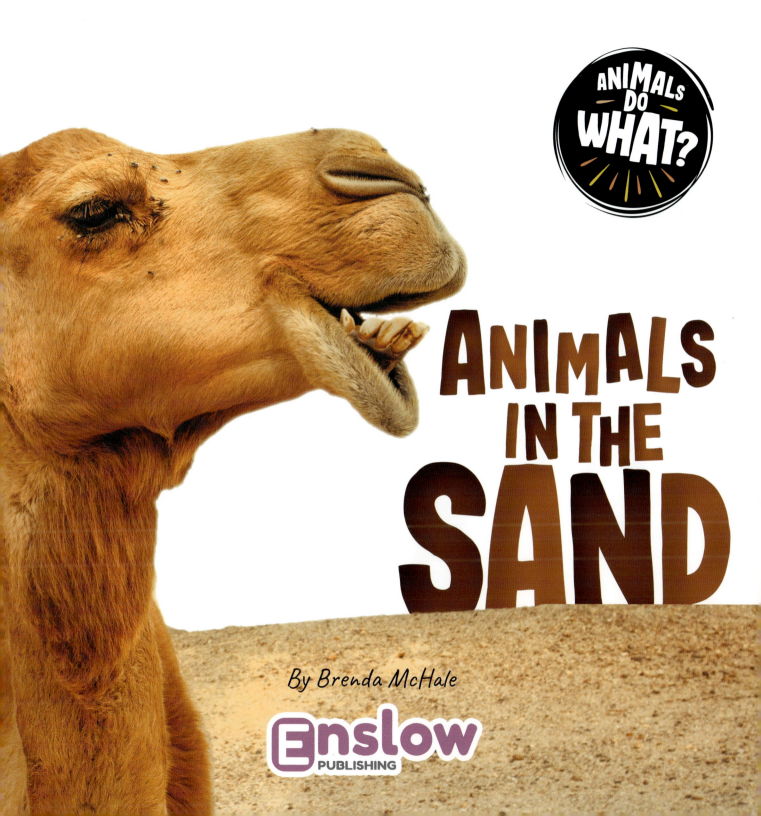

Published in 2023 by Enslow Publishing, LLC
29 East 21st Street, New York, NY 10010

© 2022 Booklife Publishing
This edition is published by arrangement with
Booklife Publishing

Edited by:
Emilie Dufresne

Designed by:
Dan Scase

All rights reserved. No part of this book may be reproduced in any form without permission in writing from the publisher, except by a reviewer.

Manufactured in the United States of America

CPSIA compliance information: Batch #CSENS23: For further information contact Enslow Publishing LLC, New York, New York at 1-800-398-2504.

Please visit our website, www.enslowpublishing.com.
For a free color catalog of all our high-quality books, call toll free 1-800-398-2504 or fax 1-877-980-4454.

Find us on

Cataloging-in-Publication Data

Names: McHale, Brenda.
Title: Animals in the sand / Brenda McHale.
Description: New York : Enslow Publishing, 2023. | Series: Animals do what? | Includes glossary and index.
Identifiers: ISBN 9781978531345 (pbk.) | ISBN 9781978531369 (library bound) | ISBN 9781978531352 (6 pack) | ISBN 9781978531376 (ebook)
Subjects: LCSH: Desert animals--Juvenile literature.
Classification: LCC QL116.M343 2023 | DDC 591.754--dc23

All images are courtesy of Shutterstock.com. With thanks to Getty Images, Thinkstock Photo and iStockphoto. Front page – Alexandra Lande. 4&5 – hagit berkovich, Viktor Loki, Pavel Krasensky, Matt Knoth. 6&7 – Carlos Amarillo, Roger de la Harpe, shflickinger. 8&9 – Roman Gilmanov, Arnoud Quanjer, OMMB, Protasov AN. 10&11 – Chantelle Bosch, Willem van de Kerkhof. 12&13 – Roger de Montfort, Earth Stories Photography. 14&15 – Shengyong Li, Vera Larina, meunierd, Anan Kaewkhammul, Inc. 16&17 – Photo by Greg Hume CC-BY-2.5, Derrick Coetzee. 18&19 – Sergei25, NATURE WEB, volkova natalia. 20&21 – Owen65, Chris Watson, Pacific Southwest Region USFWS. 22&23 – Milan Zygmunt, Ken Griffiths, Artush, Danita Delmont, Andre Coetzer.

CONTENTS

PAGE 4	**What Lives in the Sand?**
PAGE 6	**Meerkat**
PAGE 8	**Scorpion**
PAGE 10	**Shovel-Snouted Lizard**
PAGE 12	**Namaqua Chameleon**
PAGE 14	**Camel**
PAGE 16	**Honeypot Ant**
PAGE 18	**Dorcas Gazelle**
PAGE 20	**Desert Spadefoot Toad**
PAGE 22	**Wacky Wildlife**
PAGE 24	**Glossary and Index**

Words that look like this can be found in the glossary on page 24.

WHAT LIVES IN THE SAND?

It can be hard to live in the heat of the desert. But here are some types of creatures that can survive there:

Mammals such as fennec foxes

Reptiles such as short-horned lizards

Insects such as Sahara desert ants

On each page you will see a fact file like this. It will give you cool facts about the animal, such as what type of animal it is, its <u>diet</u>, and where it lives.

COYOTE

Type: Mammal
Found: North and Central America
Diet: Other small mammals

MEERKAT

Some meerkats look out for danger. They can use six different barks or whistles to tell other meerkats if there is danger.

MEERKAT
Type: Mammal
Found: Africa
Diet: Insects, lizards, and fruit

One type of whistle will tell everyone to run down to the burrow. A different whistle tells them how far away the danger is.

Meerkats sleep in a big pile to keep warm.

Meerkats can close their ears to keep the sand out.

Meerkats have an extra eyelid that covers their eyes when they dig.

When a meerkat parent needs to leave their home, a babysitter will look after the baby meerkats!

SCORPION

Some scorpions can survive up to a year without eating or drinking.

In some light, scorpions can glow in the dark.

SCORPION

Type: Arachnid
Found: Deserts, forests, and mountains
Diet: Insects, small reptiles, and animals

A baby scorpion rides on its mother's back when it's first born. But if a scorpion mother gets hungry, she might choose to eat her babies!

Scorpions that have smaller pincers are usually more <u>venomous</u>.

Small pincers

SHOVEL-SNOUTED LIZARD

The shovel-snouted lizard runs at nearly 3 feet (1 m) per second.

SHOVEL-SNOUTED LIZARD

Type: Reptile
Found: Namib desert
Diet: Small insects

NAME NOM | Animals in the Sand | NO

It dances on hot sand. It lifts two legs up, then the opposite two. This keeps its feet from overheating.

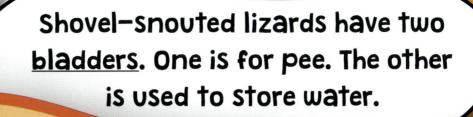

Shovel-snouted lizards have two <u>bladders</u>. One is for pee. The other is used to store water.

Other animals like to catch this lizard because it's like a water bottle for them!

NAMAQUA CHAMELEON

NAMAQUA CHAMELEON

Type: Reptile
Found: Africa
Diet: Small insects and other reptiles

NAME NOM — Animals in the Sand

In the morning, Namaqua chameleons turn dark gray. This helps them <u>absorb</u> heat from the sun to warm up.

As it gets hotter throughout the day, the chameleon turns lighter to help it stay cool.

Dark color in the morning

Light color in the heat of the day

12

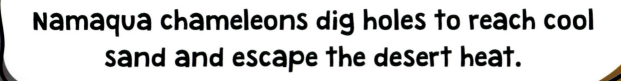

Namaqua chameleons dig holes to reach cool sand and escape the desert heat.

Its tongue is longer than its whole body, and is sticky on the end.

CAMEL

Camels say hello by blowing in each other's faces.

CAMEL

Animals in the Sand

NAME
NOM

NO

Type: Mammal
Found: Africa and Asia
Diet: Different types of plants

Camels are known for spitting up the contents of their stomachs at something that might be threatening them.

You can tell when a camel is about to spit because they huff and their cheeks bulge!

A camel can drink over 26 gallons (100 L) of water in 15 minutes. That's the same as half a bathtub full of water.

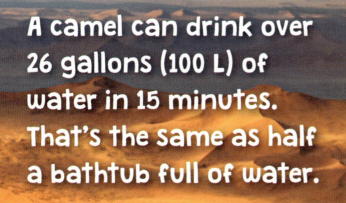

Camels moan, groan, and bellow. Some of these noises were used to create Chewbacca's voice from the *Star Wars* films!

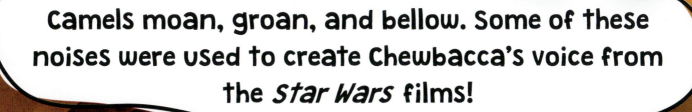

Camels can sit on really hot ground because they have thick skin on their knees and chest.

HONEYPOT ANT

HONEYPOT ANT

Type: Insect
Found: North and Central America, Africa, and Australia
Diet: Nectar and other insects

Some honeypot ants hang from the nest ceiling while other ants feed them nectar until they look like juicy grapes.

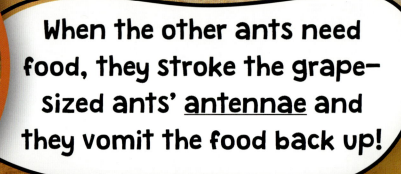

When the other ants need food, they stroke the grape-sized ants' antennae and they vomit the food back up!

Honeypot ants have been known to attack other honeypot ant colonies. They try to steal the grape-sized ants full of sugary juice.

Some people like to eat the ants as a sweet treat.

DORCAS GAZELLE

DORCAS GAZELLE

Type: Mammal
Found: Africa
Diet: Plants and small insects

Animals in the Sand

The dorcas gazelle doesn't have to pee. In very dry weather, its pee can come out as a dry lump of white stuff!

The dorcas gazelle can get all the water it needs from what it eats.

When being chased by an attacker, dorcas gazelles jump high in the air to warn other gazelles and show the attacker how fit they are.

Male dorcas gazelles make piles of poop to mark their area.

DESERT SPADEFOOT TOAD

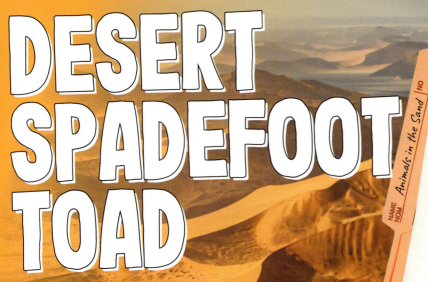

DESERT SPADEFOOT TOAD

Type: Amphibian
Found: Australia
Diet: Small creatures

The tadpoles of desert spadefoot toads sometimes eat other tadpoles in their group.

The toad's back feet are shaped like digging spades. They even have a sharp edge on them.

20

Spadefoot toad tadpoles grow very quickly, so they are ready to leave the pool they are in before it dries up in the hot desert weather.

Desert spadefoot toad tadpole

The toads dig down into the sand so that they don't get too dry. They are usually only seen aboveground after it rains.

WACKY WILDLIFE

Young tiger salamanders eat each other. But they can tell which ones are their brothers and sisters and don't eat them.

Sidewinder snakes move sideways on the sand. This is so their bodies do not touch the hot sand for too long.

GLOSSARY

absorb	to take in or soak up
amphibian	an animal that can live both on land and in water
antennae	a pair of long, thin sensors found on the heads of insects
arachnid	a type of animal that has eight legs, such as spiders and scorpions
bladders	things in animals and humans that hold pee
diet	the kinds of foods that a person or animal usually eats
insects	animals with six legs, no backbone, and usually one or two pairs of wings
mammals	animals that are warm-blooded, have a backbone, and produce milk to feed their young
nectar	a sweet liquid made by plants
nest	something made by an animal to live in and keep it safe and warm
reptiles	cold-blooded animals with scales
venomous	able to poison another animal through a bite or a scratch

INDEX

babies 7, 9, 20–22
blood 23
burrows 6
digging 7, 13, 20–21

ears 7
eyes 7, 23
legs 10
nectar 16

sand 4, 7, 10, 13, 21–23
tongues 13
water 11, 15, 18